AF408411

TWINKLE, TWINKLE, LITTLE BUG

Viktor the Viking and Pippa the Pixie: Teachable Moments in STEM

written by
Michelle Chance

illustrated by
Nadia Ronquillo

For my own pixies and Vikings,
who fill every day with adventure,
dreams, and opportunities to
learn more about the world.

Viktor and Pippa
had been playing in the forest all day,
and it was starting to get dark.

4

Viktor noticed something strange.
"Look at these bugs coming out!
They're like tiny lanterns!" Pippa giggled.
"What a beautiful light show!"

5

Pippa was a Science Pixie.
She reached out and touched a firefly.
"This is called bioluminescence," she said.
Viktor blinked. "Bio-lumi-what?"

"Bioluminescence,"
Pippa repeated.
"That's what it's called when living things
produce light. Like these fireflies!"

9

Suddenly, Viktor stopped spinning and
looked around with worry.
"Pippa, it's gotten really dark.
How will we find our way back?"

"Oh no!"
Pippa was worried too.

"We played too long.
It's too dark to see the path."

11

Pippa cupped her hands, and they began to glow.
"Maybe I can mimic the fireflies a little?"
Moths and other insects circled her.

12

Viktor laughed. "You're like a pixie lighthouse!
Why are they all coming towards you?" Viktor asked, curious.

"Some insects are attracted to light," Pippa explained.
"It helps them find food or mates. Just like the
fireflies use their glow to talk to each other."

"They think you're a giant firefly"
Viktor smiled.
"But it's not enough to be our flashlight."

13

Viktor pulled a little jar from his satchel.
"I have an idea."

Viktor began gathering the fireflies that twinkled all around them. He counted as he carefully scooped them into the jar.

"That's a great idea, Viktor!" said Pippa.
"This little lantern you've made
will help us find our way."

With Pippa's glowing hands and Viktor's firefly lantern,
they carefully walked through the forest.
On the way to the beach, they passed a cove.

Pippa exclaimed. "Look! It's not just bugs that glow.
The jellyfish are glowing too!"
Viktor leaned in for a better look.
"The water is twinkling with stars!
Why are they glowing?"

16

"Some creatures glow to find friends. Some glow to
find food. Others glow to help them hide,"
explained Pippa.
Viktor pondered this for a moment, then grinned.
"And some glow to help explorers find their way!"

Viktor and Pippa continued until they finally reached the shore.
They saw glowing waves dancing around their ship.
"Those aren't jellyfish," Viktor said, confused.
"It looks like there are lots of little glow bugs in the water."
Pippa nodded.

"There are so many glowing creatures.
There are fish and plants
and even mushrooms
that can light up!

They all glow for different reasons."

"Those are tiny creatures called plankton."
Pippa dipped a toe in the sea. "They can glow too."
"Wow," Viktor whispered in awe.
"This is even more beautiful than the dance party."

Pippa and Viktor rested near the ship, tired from their long day and the journey home. "Pippa," Viktor said finally.

"Something is wrong with the fireflies in our lantern."

They were starting to lose their light.

Pippa peered into the jar. "They need fresh air," she said. "Creatures that glow, like these fireflies, use oxygen, like the air we breathe. This mixes with a special chemical inside of them to create a tiny explosion of light! This is how fireflies twinkle.

And it's how the plankton in the water sparkle."

Viktor gently opened the jar and watched as the
fireflies blinked and flew free into the night.
"Bye-bye, fireflies!" Pippa waved.
"Thanks for lighting our way home."

The ocean and the forest seemed magical.
"The world has so many secret lights, and every glow
tells a story," Pippa mused.
Viktor smiled. "And tonight, we got to follow
that story all the way home."

I hope we learn
more tomorrow.

Materials:

1 non-toxic yellow
highlighter

Water

Flashlight

A glass jar, plastic water
bottle, or another clear
container

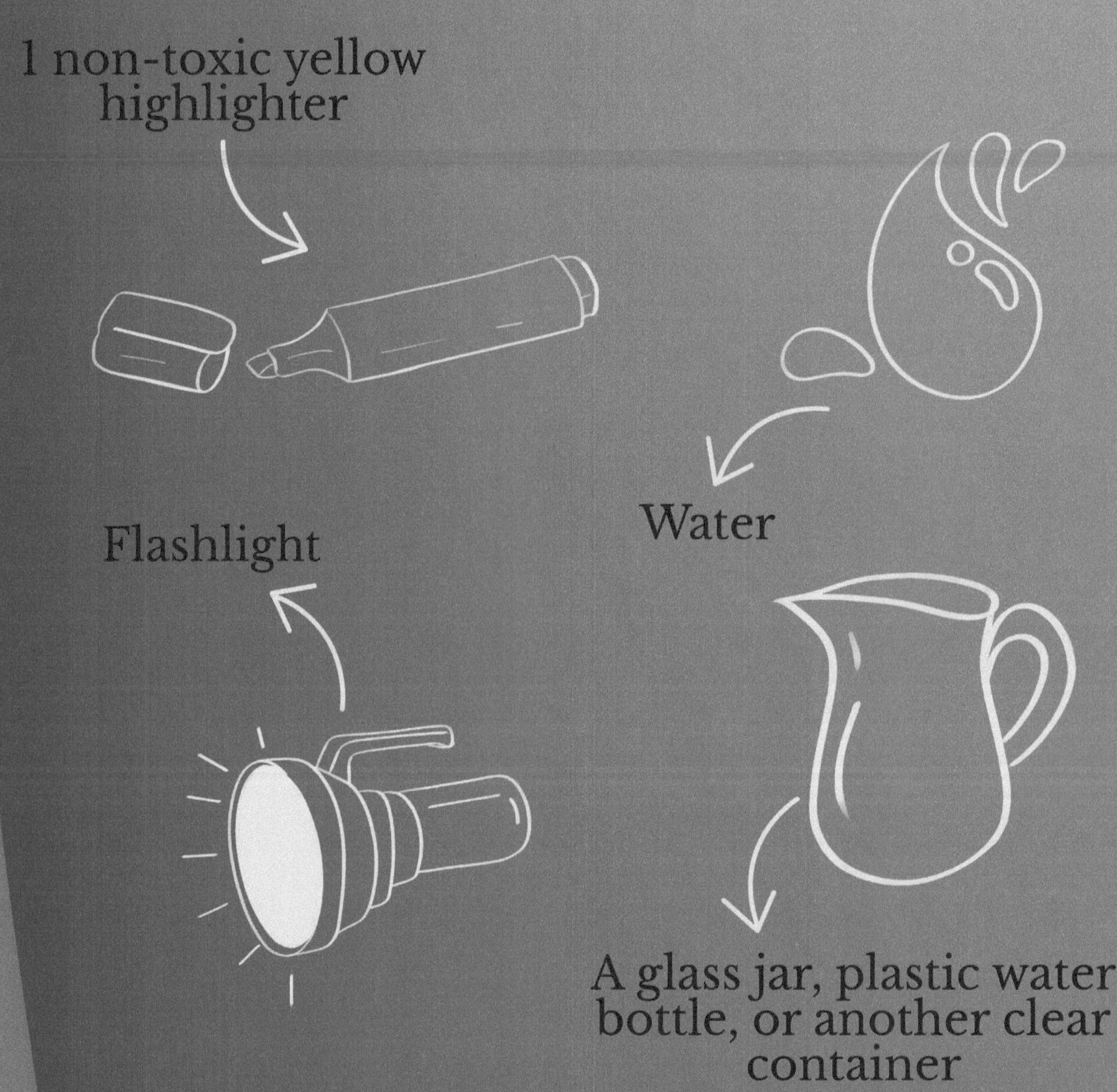

Method:

Step 1: Prepare the container.
Fill the clear container with water.

Step 2: Extract the highlighter ink.
Pop off the back of the highlighter, and pull out
the ink-soaked felt inside.

Step 3: Color the water.
Put the highlighter felt under the water, and squeeze
it until the water is stained with the highlighter ink.

Step 4: Create the glow.
Turn off the lights, and place the flashlight under
the container. Watch the water glow!

About the author:

Michelle has been intertwining the threads of science and storytelling since she could first imagine worlds beyond our own. Growing up on a farm and ranch with a pasture full of mysteries and an old typewriter, she dreamed of becoming an author. Writing took a back seat for a long time as she grew up, became a parent, and built her career. As a mom to four incredible readers, Michelle has found her greatest joy and responsibility in nurturing their questions of why? and how?.
Pippa and Viktor came to life one night in an interactive bedtime story conceived by Michelle's two youngest dreamers.
Their enthusiasm for bringing these characters from imagination to the printed page inspired not only a family project but also a realization of Michelle's lifelong dream. Dressed in their pixie and Viking costumes, her children embarked on real-life science experiments, breathing life into the adventures that now fill the pages of these books.

Away from storytelling, Michelle has carved a
successful path in the tech industry, where she advocates
for STEM education and works to ignite a passion for science
and engineering in the next generation. Her journey from a
young girl fascinated by the mysteries of the universe to a
technology professional and a children's author is a testament
to the power of curiosity, imagination, and the relentless
pursuit of knowledge.

Through her stories, Michelle hopes to inspire young readers
to explore, question, and dream. She believes that within every
child lies a scientist and an adventurer ready to discover the
wonders of the world. With a heart full of stories and a mind
eager to solve the puzzles of the universe, Michelle invites
you and your little ones to join Pippa and Viktor on a journey
where magic and science meet, crafting a world where the
quest for knowledge is the greatest adventure of all.